T0065766

Choosing *Your* Words Wisely

Principles for Effective Communication and Conflict Resolution

DALE BARRETT

WESTBOW
PRESS°
A DIVISION OF THOMAS NELSON
& ZONDERVAN

WestBow Press books may be ordered through booksellers or by contacting:

WestBow Press
A Division of Thomas Nelson & Zondervan
1663 Liberty Drive
Bloomington, IN 47403
www.westbowpress.com
844-714-3454

ISBN: 978-1-6642-8133-2 (sc)
ISBN: 978-1-6642-8134-9 (e)

Library of Congress Control Number: 2022919272

Print information available on the last page.

WestBow Press rev. date: 11/2/2022

Introduction

Words are the indispensable means of human communication. Whether verbalized or written, they impact every arena of life. Potentially words can inform, affirm, and encourage for good, or they can criticize, disparage, and destroy for bad. The Bible addresses this apparent conundrum in James 3:10 with these words: "From the same mouth come blessing and cursing ... these things ought not to be so."

James has acknowledged some critical things about the tongue in this insightful biblical passage, summarizing it by saying a "restless evil, full of deadly poison" (James 3:8). James concludes that "no human being can tame the tongue" (James 3:8). In the following chapter, James asks, "What causes quarrels and what causes fights among you? Is it not this, that your passions are at war within you?" (James 4:1). With these words we are reminded of the inevitable link between internal emotional conflict and external acting out in both our words and our behavior.

This assessment would seem to be without remedy, as if we are remanded to a life of emotional and behavioral volatility compounded by the negative words we use that are both damaging and destructive. Fueling our sense of frustration is our daily inundation of belligerent words in our political dialogue and news media. We hear the same in our television programs and the movies we watch as well as in the music we listen to and the books we read—all of this in search of information and entertainment as a viable part of our daily regimen.

The trickle-down effect of "bad words" seeps into every corner and crevice of our lives. It impacts our workspace, the realm of close personal friendships, and tragically, the ideally safe and sacred family dynamic. Family members become estranged, husbands and wives are displaced, resulting in the continued high rate of broken homes and divorce. There are countless reasons why marriages and families are in crisis, but none, I believe, more significant than the breakdown in communication and conflict resolution skills.

It would be arrogant and simplistic to infer that the reading of this book could fix any or all of that. Even to submit some formulaic solution or to suggest some prescribed program as a panacea for this communication crisis would be foolhardy. Why then would I even attempt to address this burgeoning crisis when solutions seem doomed by the biblical proclamation "No man can tame the tongue"?

Wisdom is needed. *Wisdom is seeing things from God's point of view.* Here is a key passage from James in the context of his words about the tongue:

Who is wise and understanding among you? By his conduct let him show his works in the meekness of wisdom. But if you have bitter jealousy and selfish ambition in your hearts, do not boast and be false to the truth. This is not the wisdom that comes from above, but is earthly, unspiritual, and demonic. For where jealousy and selfish ambition exist there will be disorder and every vile practice. But the wisdom from above is first pure, then peaceable, gentle, open to reason, full of mercy and good fruits, impartial and sincere. And a harvest of righteousness is sown by those who make peace. (James 3:13–18)

These verses articulate several important things that are foundational for this book.

1. Wisdom and understanding are highly desirable.
2. Our conduct (words and deeds) reflects our wisdom, or lack of it.
3. Jealousy and selfish ambition are twin roots of unwise and evil conduct (words and deeds).
4. Wisdom "from above" is reflected in the good fruit it bears.
5. Those who make peace sow and reap a harvest of righteousness (right living).

What then are principles for "right living" that can instruct our communication, specifically the words we use? What would/could happen if we were to *choose our words wisely* in our relationships with each other—especially in marriage?

Ephesians 4:25–32 is a platform for identifying seven key principles that can guide how we choose our words and how we can guard and grow the critical relationships of our lives. This is a part of my own journey as a man, husband, father, pastor, counselor, and friend. I hope you will join me with the hopeful expectation that *choosing your words wisely* can dramatically impact the relationship landscape of your life.

1

Speak the truth in love.

—EPHESIANS 4:15, 24

The goal of confrontation is reconciliation.

I am by nature a peacemaker. I want to keep everyone happy and will work hard to broker peace between others and me. I am convinced that *the goal of confrontation is reconciliation.*

Sometimes during an argument I am silent—as if ignoring a hurt or a feeling of anger will simply make it go away. I have discovered the hard way that this only delays the inevitable—a burgeoning uneasiness within or, ultimately, a moment of displaced anger. For the sake of understanding my use of the term *displaced anger,* I define it as a moment when an angry reaction to a situation is more intense than the situation would seem to deserve. What happens in that moment is that because there is unprocessed anger stored away, it gets triggered in a moment of conflict or confrontation. What spews forth is the combination of the past hurt and the present. Many of us have experienced that moment when we asked ourselves, "Where did that come from?"

There is an obvious danger in this dynamic of how we process (or do not) our emotions in a conflict, especially with spouses or close friends. We want to protect and preserve these relationships because they are vital to our emotional and relational health. The failure to deal with deep emotions can come back to haunt us. The reality is when we subconsciously store away these feelings, we can unwittingly lay the ground for resentment and bitterness. The Bible warns against that with these words:

> Strive for peace with everyone … see to it …
> that no root of bitterness springs up and causes
> trouble, and by it many become defiled.
> (Hebrews 12:14–15)

Bitterness can take root, make us miserable, and impact the quality of our relationship with others—even those not a part of the cause for it.

As a result, the decision to ignore our anger is not healthy. Later we will talk more about the options available in processing our anger. But for now, let us agree that ignoring our anger and our hurts is not conducive to nurturing and maintaining good relationships.

Why then do we choose to not respond in a moment when we are emotionally impacted in a negative, painful way? Or why is it when we do choose to respond, what comes out only serves to accelerate the tension of the moment? Because that is what frequently happens. We are often reluctant to share our true feelings. In marriage, that can become a contributing factor to a diminished relationship. In friendships, it can signal separation and withdrawal. In business relationships, it can hamper helpful dialogue between coworkers or create disruptive distance between a boss and his or her employees.

Choosing your words wisely is the theme of this book, and it provides a constructive path to responsible, healthy confrontation. The by-product of this can facilitate the opportunity for reconciliation.

Let me illustrate the importance of this principle with an imaginary scenario. Often when this husband comes home from a long day at work, he gives his wife a perfunctory kiss on the cheek, falls into his easy chair, and buries his head in his cell phone. He is processing his day at work and making sure that his emails are caught up and his calendar for the next day is set. His wife has been busy cleaning house and running errands for grandchildren during the day and is in the process of preparing a late dinner. It has been a long day for both. She calls her husband to dinner. He comes willingly but notices that when he tries to make conversation, she seems distant.

"So your day must have been rough? What happened?" he asks.

"Just another day. Nothing major," she responds with a dismissive tone in her voice.

They dig into their chicken potpies, but it is quiet. Too quiet. The truth is that this is a frequent occurrence, a constant of their life that she has addressed. Only last week she had said to him, "Let me know when you are available," after he had slipped into his familiar postwork liturgy. She said it with a hint of sarcasm, and he simply grunted and said, "I'm busy right now." It was not the first time. And their dinner was quiet and uneasy, as it often was.

What is going on in this seemingly innocuous scenario? Should it even matter? The answer is a resounding yes. Both have allowed themselves to settle into a pattern or cycle of behavior that accelerates the distance between them—a natural function of their necessarily separate spheres of life— and they have not learned how to merge these two spheres in a noncombative way. The occasional attempts that she makes are clipped sentences wrapped in passive aggressiveness, and his responses are equally disconnected from what is really in focus here for her. *What priority and place do I have in your life?* she has inwardly conceded. *It doesn't matter. He will always be who he is and work will always be first, even though he's supposed to be semiretired.* At this point, it is a deep hurt that has been buried away and become a point of resentment. Dinners have become a regimen of sitting across the table and awkward silence, a silence to which they have acquiesced and become accustomed.

There is another principle at work here. *There is a significant difference between resignation and resolution.* Case in point, they have become resigned to this reality:

- Tom will always work when he comes home.
- Dinner together will always be an insignificant event.
- And it's not worth trying to fix it. Besides, when it has been addressed, it has been dismissed. He does not get it. She is done hoping that it can be different.

Resolution is not allowing resignation to set in, thus fueling the potential for resentment and bitterness. The truth is, resigned as she is to the dinner dynamic, she dreads it. Even preparation has become routine, and the meals have become banal and ordinary. She has lost the joy she once experienced as a creative cook. What if she was instead resolved to preserve the evening meal as a meaningful time of reconnecting with him? What could she do differently that might change the texture of their evening together? What if she simply said, "I'm not giving up. This is too important for me and for us"?

Let us think specifically about some guidelines in approaching a confrontational conversation.

1. What is the *goal of confrontation* for her? Is it simply to dump her feelings of abandonment and insignificance on him? Is it to rehearse a litany of all the things that he does (or does not do) that enhance this feeling of insecurity about her place in his life?

2. If her *intentional goal is reconciliation*—to be drawn back into close relationship with him—then the words she chooses will be vastly different from if her motivation is primarily to get this off her chest.

3. Assuming the reconciliation goal, *timing and tone matter*. When is the best time to have this conversation? In what setting can she get his maximum attention? Can she say this as an expression of her love for him, or will she scold him and raise her voice because that's how she has learned to get his attention?

4. What is a *healthy functional goal* for her? And how will she express it in a way he will hear it and potentially embrace it?

Here is an example of what that conversation might look like: "Honey, after dinner, can we go for a walk? I would like to share some things I've been thinking about, and it's been a long time since we've walked in the neighborhood together." She knows he loves evening walks. His hopeful response is "Sure, we can do that."

As they walk, it is important that she does not dive into confrontational dialogue but that she identifies something positive as a point of positive connection. "I know you would have loved our son's basketball game. He made two baskets and a free throw. I told him you would have loved to have been there but you were working."

He understood. "Thanks for reminding him about my work. I am glad you were able to go for both of us. You said you had been thinking about some things. I'm listening."

"I have been thinking about our lives and how busy we are and how I want to guard the time we get to have together. Last night when you came home, I know you were tired. You headed straight for your chair, grabbed your cell phone, and went back to work. I guess in that moment, I felt unimportant and ignored. We have talked about it before, but we seem to have fallen into this routine and I have come to dread dinnertime. I used to look forward to this time of reconnecting, and it is just not happening. What could I do to make that time together at dinner something to look forward to and a time when we can reconnect?"

She could have opted for "I have given up trying to get your attention at dinnertime. You are more married to your work than you are to me."

And his reaction would probably be one of defensiveness and avoidance. "I can't believe you would say that when you know how tired I am and how hard I am working to pay our bills."

And the cycle would have continued, each defending his or her own territory without an investment in the other's.

His response to her "speaking the truth in love" is critical. He is, hopefully, willing now to enter dialogue with this conversation characterized as an appeal for quality time together. "I am hearing you. I know when I get home my head is in another world. I do not mean to ignore you, but I have a hard time putting my work aside. I will join in with you in making the dinner time a special time. How could I help? It is important to me too." Tom is choosing his words wisely because his goal is to be reconciled—not estranged—from his wife.

Dialogue about the details can follow because choosing words carefully has allowed for a time to express feelings, to listen well and validate the other's concern, potentially setting the table for conflict resolution. The conversation above may seem contrived to you—too rehearsed and unnatural. That is because it probably is. It is hard to respond—not react—without disciplined intentionality. *The difference between responding and reacting is time*—taking time to filter our reactive feelings—and to respond in a way that enables—not short-circuits—constructive healing dialogue. Learning how to do this because we value our relationships will help us break out of self-indulgent patterns of behavior practicing a perspective identified in the Bible as "looking not only at our own interests but at the interests of others" (Philippians 2:4).

"Speaking the truth in love" feels like an oxymoron—as if "love" and "truth" are not easily wed together. When confronted with truth—truth that exposes some shortfall or demands some response—it is difficult not to become defensive. We can bridle our tongues or compartmentalize our anger for a while. Often it is to our own detriment, however, allowing each reoccurrence of the unaddressed offense to trigger a potentially more volatile reaction. When we can take it no longer, an explosive encounter may take place and both parties may be surprised by the intensity of that moment. Failure to speak out about our hurts and offenses creates fertile ground for estrangement—emotional and sometimes physical. "I don't even want to be around someone who doesn't care enough for me to put down his work when he comes home so that we can have time to be reconnect. Why are we even married?" That's a dangerous place for her to pitch her tent. And where did it all begin? Several months before, when he came home from work and repeatedly failed to engage her. He occupied space with her but was not present. He moved from hurt to anger to passive aggressiveness to confrontation. Thankfully, rather than being resigned to a simmering resentment, she chose to invest in the reconciliation her heart longed for and practiced healing dialogue with him by choosing her words wisely.

I wish I could say this is a foolproof strategy and that reconciliation is always achieved. With friends these kinds of conversations are often couched in terms of the potential value we assign to the maintenance of the relationship. With coworkers where the requirement for survival is not necessarily that we be friends, we can slip into a reluctant management of the relationship—doing just enough to get our work done. But if we must spend forty hours a week together, is there not value to be gained by asking, "Can we talk? I sense there is something between us and I would like to own what part of that belongs to me. What can I do to make our relationship work?" That in contrast to "What's wrong with you? Did you get up on the wrong side of the bed this morning?" Incidentally, if you know it is on you, it is more honest to say, "I know I overreacted a couple of weeks ago at lunch and I am sorry. What can I do to make it right?"

In my fifty-plus years of counseling I have observed the

hardening of hearts in relationships that were once close and intimate. Often the parties have abandoned their right to say what they are feeling. *A goal of communication in marriage should be seeking to provide a safe place to honestly share our feelings.* The caveat is that even if we don't say it with words, we will eventually communicate it through body language. The inevitable painful result is the explosion of hurtful words or the painful absence of words in the daily dialogue of life together.

The biblical context for "speaking the truth in love" is set when Paul wrote, "Putting away falsehood, let each one of you speak the truth with his neighbor for we are members of one another." Earlier he had simply written, "Speaking the truth in love, we are to grow up in very way" (Ephesians 4:15, 25). Paul addressed the first-century church at Ephesus and taught the importance of integrity and truthfulness with each another because the bonds of meaningful relationships demand it. This is a challenge for our personal growth and maturity— especially in marriage where we are identified as "one flesh." This is how we appropriate the grace God gives us to live and "grow up" with one another.

I am asking you to honestly consider these questions:

- Is it safe to tell my spouse how I really feel?
- Do I provide an environment for my spouse to freely and safely express his/her feelings?
- Is there something I have become resigned to in a relationship that matters?

- Do I dread work because there is unresolved friction between a coworker and me and I have been unwilling to do my part in seeking reconciliation?
- Is there a settled bitterness and resentment in my heart because I am continuing to nurse relationship wounds I have been unwilling to address?

The goal of confrontation is reconciliation. If that is your goal, you will choose your words wisely. Some people ask me if it would be better to write out what they are feeling and present it in a letter. The reasons for considering this option would include a careful evaluation of what you are preparing to say (maybe "sleeping on it") and presenting it in a format where reactions are delayed—allowing for responses to be more carefully considered as emotions are processed. The objections to remember are that there is something about "speaking the truth in love" that is dually conveyed in words and in facial language that a letter struggles to convey. In situations where a wife has felt unsafe in such confrontations, I have sometime suggested a careful and prayerfully written communication of her feelings that meet the criterion of speaking in love and seeking reconciliation as the compelling motivations. Some men have a difficult time confronting the emotions of others; statistical data suggests they are more likely to discount emotional factors and to err on the side of logic. (That's my defense.) In any case, there is no acceptable substitute for loving and honest confrontation when misunderstanding, hurt, and pain have been experienced. Emotional assaults on relationship, if ignored and unaddressed, will eventually come to light and the context in which these feelings are exposed may be too painful or too late to remedy.

I began this book with the principle *the goal of confrontation is reconciliation.* I am convinced it is foundational for the following reasons:

1. Conflict in inevitable.
2. Confrontation is difficult.
3. Responding versus reacting is critical.
4. The goal of confrontation shapes the way we choose to communicate.
5. If reconciliation is the goal, "speaking the truth in love" is the path to follow.

Hopefully, this will get us off to a good start in thinking about how we can use our words effectively in a pattern of communication that draws us closer to each other, not pushes us further apart.

2

Be angry and do not sin.

—EPHESIANS 4:26, 31

*The appropriate processing of anger is an
integral part of the communication process.*

As a young man, I wrestled with an unruly temper. My early propensity for anger was fueled by competing in basketball at a small college and, later, in multiple venues until I was fifty-six years old. In the early days, it was just the identity thing. "Am I or am I not a good (if not great) competitive basketball player?" It morphed into "Is this really the best way to keep off weight?" and then to "How long can I keep on doing this without embarrassing myself?" When my doctor suggested that I was jeopardizing my ambulatory future, I quit. On the spot. That created a whole other level of internalized anger (i.e., "I can't believe I can't compete any longer.") There are still fleeting moments that I grieve the end of my basketball "career," but they are no longer punctuated by anger.

These days I do not get angry easily. Part of that is a function of age, but I would like to think it is because I have learned and am learning how to appropriately process my anger. The Bible uses words like "anger," "wrath," "bitterness," and "malice" in the Ephesian's passage that is the basis on our seven key principles governing how we communicate with one another. I want to distinguish them from each other in this simple way: "Anger" is the initial feeling, and it can be as innocuous as "a strong feeling of being upset or annoyed because of something wrong or bad" (Webster). "Wrath"—a more intense word—signifies a "strong vengeful anger or indignation." For our purposes, it is often "stored anger" or "unprocessed anger." "Bitterness" is the cumulative feeling of something "distasteful or distressing to the mind," and as such can be the unavoidable result of failing to address deep emotions like anger and wrath. "Malice" is "the desire to cause pain, injury, or distress to another" and is often anger acted our vengefully or bitterly.

I see an unintended chronology in these words, connected to each other and reflective of the process of ignoring anger or addressing it ineffectively or inadequately. Here is my thought about the relationship and chronology of these words: Anger is the initial feeling; when dismissed or ignored (and stored), it becomes wrath. Wrath, unaddressed, potentially results in bitterness (and resentment) and sadly, sometimes malice or anger acted out. These words are all used in the biblical contest where communication and conflict resolution are in view and understanding this key principle about processing anger is critical to how well we relate to one another.

Let me illustrate by telling you the story of another married couple. He is a successful businessman and met his wife after both had gone through painful divorces. Both single for several years, they connected over an office remodeling project (her office, his construction business) and eighteen months later were married. She had come from an abusive relationship, and Ron, though successful in business, admitted his history of relational communication issues in their premarital counseling.

The first few months of their marriage were like the proverbial honeymoon season until one night after dinner he asked, "Are you going to clean up this place before you go to bed?"

Both spouses had full-time jobs so the singular "you" and the not-so-subtle hint of sarcasm coupled with a tone of condescension sat poorly with her. But she chose to ignore it—though she felt both anger and hurt—and dutifully cleaned up the house before coming to bed.

When they awakened in the morning, everything seemed normal. He was his usual "Have a good day. See you tonight" self, and she reluctantly hugged him as he left, still feeling a tinge of anger from the night before.

All seemed well enough until a few weeks later, as they

were preparing to go out with friends for dinner, he blurted out, "Do we need to think about hiring a housekeeper?" Not waiting for an answer, he rushed to the car to get to the dinner engagement on time. His wife was stunned by the question and reeling inside when she slipped into the front seat. In her first marriage, her husband had often publicly berated her for her lack of orderliness and disdainfully said to his friends, "I certainly didn't marry her for her housekeeping skills." She had dismissed those words because they paled in comparison to his daily assaults on her for the failure at almost every task she attempted—from the clothes she wore to her makeup, the meals she prepared, and her "lack of attention to details," as he summarized it again and again.

Her husband now would never say something like that to her friends, and occasionally he would compliment her for a good meal or how great she looked. Still, his comments hurt, but she determined they were nothing compared to what she experienced in her first marriage so she pushed them back into the corner of her mind reserved for "things too painful to address."

One night, when both were tired and he had asked for the umpteenth time, "When are you going to get it together in keeping the house clean?" she exploded. "I will when you decide to help me!" She was surprised about how much venom and volume accompanied those few words. What followed was an angry exchange and his decision to sleep on the sofa once he cleared a place to lie on it.

The next morning was awkwardly quiet, and the regimen

of "Have a good day. See you tonight" with the perfunctory hug was performed quickly and coldly. She was beginning to recognize some feelings of bitterness and resentment, and he, surprised by her response, concluded to himself, "I should have expected this; her parents' home is a mess!"

When he returned home that night, the house was clean and orderly and a bill for $200 from "Your Friendly Maid Service," a local house cleaning agency, was on the desk where the bills were placed. The conversation about this increase in monthly expenditures was strained.

You know the rest of the story, right? There was never healthy dialogue about who should clean the house and how it was a shared responsibility. As a result, the distance between them intensified as their anger, now turned to wrath, was reflected in bitterness acted out in unkind behavior toward each other.

And all of this over a messy house?

No. All of this was about a failure to communicate and an unwillingness to process layers of anger and hurt. This seems innocent enough, but it is illustrative of what happens in relationships that matter when we fail to address our emotions and share our feelings.

What then are the ways we should address anger? I think it is safe to assume that even in the best of relationships we get hurt and anger is fueled by the stuff of daily interaction, even though often unintended. There are four ways we commonly deal with anger and hurt. We *repress* it, we *suppress* it, we *express* it, or we *confess* it. Understanding these four ways will enable us to choose our words wisely when we are attempting to communicate how we feel.

The easiest thing for most of us to do in response to conflict and personal affront is to *repress* anger. The word *repress* is defined as "the restraint, prevention of a feeling" (Oxford). Feelings are not sinful in and of themselves; in fact, the command "Be angry and sin not" (Ephesians 4:25) argues that point. This wife's initial response to her husband's pronouncement "Are you going to clean up this place before you go to bed?"—a statement more than a question because no dialogue is expected—is one of expected hurt. Not that he intended that, but in his frustration, he reacts unkindly, seeking to achieve a result because he too has been repressing his true feelings about the condition of the house. Now it erupts in this unsavory way.

Her decision is to keep how she feels inside. It may be that she is surprised—if not shocked—by her husband's words; in any case, she chooses not to react or respond overtly. Notice that word *overtly*. There is an internal response—hurt, pain, anger, surprise, shock—but it remains locked up within her. She cleans up the house dutifully but, as time will reveal, begrudgingly. And in burying these feelings, she is adding to a preexistent reservoir of hurt. Remember her story? Her first husband had publicly embarrassed her more than once with sarcastic remarks about her inefficiency as a housekeeper. He had ultimately divorced her and, predictably, she carried this baggage into this new marriage. As a result, her internal response is triggered not only by her husband's words but by a history of stored hurt and bitterness from her first marriage.

It seems strange that both can awaken the next day and live as if nothing has happened—as if the words spoken accomplished their purpose because she cleaned the house. There is no discussion, no expressions of emotions, just a perfunctory return to life as normal. But it is not without impact.

Words—our most common way of expressing ourselves—have impact, intended or not. In times of conflict and duress, we may not choose our words wisely. Maybe it is because we do not know what to say, or it may even be true that when we have chosen to respond verbally we have been dismissed and unheard. As a result, we have mistakenly assumed it is simply better to say nothing.

There is something to be said for the delay in responding—choosing not to react—and we will discuss that further later. But to ignore or dismiss hurtful words in the interest of not making a scene, or "opening a hornet's nest," is to lay the foundation for expanding discomfort and duress.

A second way to handle hurt is to *suppress* our feelings. This is closely related to repression, but in the realm of conflict resolution, it is chronologically a further step in communication dysfunction. Suppression is to "consciously inhibit or avoid considering" something (Oxford), and it carries the idea of intentionally forcing the thought or memory from evaluation or discussion.

When this wife hears her husband's words the first time,

it is almost a reflexive response for her to say nothing, given her personal history and pain. She does not even think for a moment of saying anything to him; she simply does her "duty" and cleans the house. But there is no permanent long-term commitment to her household duties—no conversation about what these words meant and what the resolution for this is ongoing. With no resolution—no observation by her husband of the effort made—the seeds of bitterness and continuing conflict are sown.

The stalemate leads to further confrontation by her husband, who now suggests they hire someone to do the cleaning, but he does not wait for a response, nor does he have any apparent interest in discussing the situation. For him, he simply belches out his unhappiness in these unkind words, unwilling to choose wisely words that will allow for conversation and helpful feedback geared to a mutually satisfying solution. She has been nursing her hurt and must now work harder not to react. She suppresses her anger because it is too painful for her to challenge him and to address her feelings about this subject in general regarding his dictatorial pronouncements about what she needs to do.

Because both spouses are inappropriately processing their feelings (if at all), this situation—seemingly benign—is accelerating in its intensity, assuming a greater impact than either expected. He chooses to react without dialogue by issuing unilateral statements that reflect his sentiments, assuming she will get the hint. On the other hand, she represses and suppresses her feelings because the history of hurt she carries—now retriggered by his edict—fuels more than she is willing to address. Because of his penchant for not listening, she consciously decides not to share how she feels, wrongfully assuming this is the better way.

Repressing our feelings may seem appropriate as we gather ourselves and take time to evaluate the content of what we have heard. But to fail to acknowledge this pain—even if reflectively later—is dangerous. Now recurrent triggering comments—if ignored or repressed—lay the subconscious foundation for suppression: a forceful deliberate decision to not discuss how we feel with our spouse. Often this decision is because we have become *resigned* to how things are, how things generally go when we do have conversations. Here is an important principle to remember: *resignation lays the ground for bitterness.*

It is imperative that in conflict management we choose resolution, not resignation. Instead of accepting things as they are and ignoring and/or nursing the woundedness of painful words—resigning ourselves to the imagined hopelessness of change—we should be *resolved* to intentionally pursue reconciliation. Relationships are worth that!

In the next chapter, we will consider the options of expression and confession to deepen our understanding of how to choose our words wisely.

3

Do not let then sun go down on your anger.

—EPHESIANS 4:26, 31

*Keep short accounts so that your communication
is not undermined by unresolved issues.*

One of my favorite verses from the Bible is "Don't let the sun go down on your anger" (Ephesians 4:26, 31). My personal paraphrase is "Don't go to bed angry." Implicit in that verse is the reality of the potential harm that comes from unprocessed anger.

Though repressing and suppressing our emotions may seem normative and a way to manage how we feel by not addressing our true feelings and emotions, we must acknowledge that ignoring our hurt and pain does not make them go away. What then are our options? How do we address our painful experiences in life with one another that have conflict written into them? How can choosing our words wisely make a difference?

One obvious way is *expressing* our feelings. This seems at first glance simplistic. From our illustration of in the previous chapter, one might suggest that the husband was merely expressing his feelings when he said to his wife, "Are you going to clean up this place before you go to bed?" Notice a few problematic things about the expressions of his feelings.

1. Timing. It is immediately following dinner—after both had come home from a busy day of work—that he issues this "you" directive.
2. Tone. It has the hint of sarcasm and condescension and is not really meant to invite any kind of constructive dialogue.
3. Intent. It is meant to precipitate a behavioral response and is implicitly a demand—not an opportunity for dialogue with the goal of resolution.

If expressing our feelings means simply making unfiltered statements about how we feel, this fails to meet the standard of choosing our words wisely. These kinds of unilateral declarations tend to only provide momentary release for the one enunciating his/her feelings. Because they are unfiltered, they have the inverse effect of clearing the air; instead, they muddy the waters.

As he continues to express his feelings, each successive statement seems more lethal (i.e., "Do we need to think about hiring a housekeeper?" and "When are you going to get it together in keeping the house clean?") Remember the context of the first question. They are on their way to dinner with friends and Ron does not wait for an answer as he jumps into the car. In the second instance, before climbing into bed after a busy day, he asks a recurrent question—one apparently never open for discussion—and his wife explodes. Remember the wording of his question. "When are *you* going to get it together?" He has not learned that a question formed in that timing with that tone without intent for mutual resolution is not conducive to harmony and change.

She, on the other hand, having ignored any attempt to verbally respond in situations like this before, now shouts out, "I will when you decide to help me!" She is surprised by the amount of emotion that accompanies her response. What she does not realize is that in her seemingly disproportionate response, she is exhibiting a form of displaced anger.

Often when emotion expressed seems disproportionate to the situation, it is displaced or it is anger triggered in the moment by the incident in focus adding to and exposing a backlog of unprocessed (stored) anger (wrath) with connective tissue to the moment in time. The reality is that she has never dealt with the abuse of her first husband's condescending behavior and now, even though her new husband's behavior may seem only a facsimile of it, it triggers what has never been dealt with. It is not solely his fault, but he unwittingly fuels her anger because he has not chosen his words wisely.

Expressing our feelings is always a healthy option if we do it with a filter. Here is a reminder of an important truth from chapter 1 that should characterize our attempts at dealing with conflict—the goal of confrontation is reconciliation. "Speaking the truth in love" is the biblical concomitant of this truth. Expressing our feelings can include a wide array of unacceptable options, such as screaming, using expletives, throwing something, and punching a wall. We would all agree that these are not constructive options for communicating how we feel. They are expressive but do not meet the gold standard of reconciliation.

It is important to note that there are other inappropriate ways we communicate our feelings. Sometimes it is with body language—a scowl, a cold shoulder, leaving a room abruptly without warning, etc. It can also be done in passive aggressive behavior whereby what we do is purposely designed to communicate our displeasure or unhappiness, without verbalizing it.

Given then the potential shortfall of merely expressing our feelings, what is our best option in dealing with anger and conflict? I want to suggest the word *confessing* in effectively addressing our anger. This may represent a departure from your way of thinking and, admittedly, has a basis in biblical understanding, but it effectively describes how we best communicate our feelings.

There are several definitions of the word *confess* that relate to the biblical understanding of the Word. Whereas the common understanding is to "admit or acknowledge something reluctantly because one feels slightly ashamed or embarrassed" (Oxford Dictionary), there are different connotations in the Greek word used in the New Testament, *homologeo*. In the classical Greek, it meant to "say the same thing, to agree, admit and acknowledge" and was used often in a legal context of signing documents. It morphed in the biblical context to an "owning up to something you know and telling it forthrightly" (Simply Bible). Thus, confessing one's sin (1 John 1:9) was the ownership of one's feelings and/or failures and declaring them honestly. The intent here was to be restored to a right relationship with God.

Confessing our anger—for that matter, any of our feelings—as an act of taking ownership of them and expressing them honestly with the goal of preserving or being restored to a right relationship is a constructive way for processing our emotions.

How would that have worked in our couple's communication? What if he had said, "Sweetheart, what can we do together to get the house clean? I know I am probably the fussy one, but I feel better when things are in order"? Notice that this has the mutual "we" and infers his participation so it does not feel like a unilateral edict. Additionally, he could confess or *own* his feelings about things being in disorder.

Another way he could have responded is this: "I know we both are busy and we both want a clean house. How can we do this together?" In this instance, he makes a distinction between *motive* and *methodology*. Instead of saying, "I guess I am the only one who wants a clean house"—inferring a less noble motive on her part—he assumes she wants the same, believing the best about her.

First Corinthians 13:4–7, in giving some descriptive phrases about the operation of love, states, "Love believes the best," or it assumes the best of the person who is loved. The converse of this would be to say, "If you really loved me, you would do a better job of cleaning the house." Here motive is on trial, and since motive is a factor of one's character, it is difficult not to respond defensively, short-circuiting the prospect of productive dialogue.

If the focus is methodology—and there are multiple ways of doing things, sometimes more than one good way—then character is not in focus and the presumption of mutual intent for good paves the way for discussion of differing approaches to how to get something done. Admittedly, those conversations can be difficult as well, but they are destined for a better end because they are not about personal assault.

Let us examine this idea from the wife's perspective. When she heard her husband's sarcastic remark about her housecleaning, what if she had said, "Honey, I know how important keeping a clean house is to you, and I am sorry I drop the ball in this area. I am so tired when I get home from work that I struggle to make this a priority"? Now she is *validating* his feelings, not defending hers but giving context to the issue for her.

She might also have said, "I know this is a big issue and I care about it too, but I feel really demeaned and unappreciated when you say things like this as if its only my responsibility." Here is ownership of her feelings in a nonjudgmental way as well as an acknowledgment of his concerns. This does not mean there will not be some struggle and "arm wrestling" in the conversation that follows, but it provides a platform for working toward a solution together.

All of this may sound contrived and unrealistic in the flow of everyday life. Choosing your words takes effort, but if the investment we make in one another is geared to protect and preserve our relationship, it seems a small price to pay.

Keep short accounts. Do not repress and suppress your feelings; in that moment, express them (with a filter) and, better yet, confess them. Own them. Do so with the intent of not allowing anger to get a foothold in your relationship. Ephesians 4:27 says, "And give no opportunity to the devil."

When my wife and I have a had an unsettling argument or a sharp disagreement and we are carrying some of that anger to bed with us, I often turn to her and say, "This is not about whether or not I love you. We will find a way to resolve this." It is hard to stay angry when we choose our words wisely.

CHAPTER

4

Let no corrupting talk come out of your mouths but only such as is good for building up.

—EPHESIANS 4:29

*Communication should always be constructive
in the pursuit of conflict resolution.*

Dealing with anger is essential to effecting meaningful communication. On the front side, however, the appropriate question might be "How can we communicate in a manner that limits the painful pattern and cycle of anger in the relationships we value?" For that matter, how do we diminish the opportunity for the fueling and simulation of anger in our daily interactions? It is the right question in the same way the consideration of how to prevent the occurrence of cancer is married to how to effectively treat it.

The inevitability of anger and emotion in our interactions is borne out by this scriptural question:

> What causes quarrels and what causes fight among you? Is it not this that your passions are at work within you? You desire and do not have, so you murder. You covet and cannot obtain, so you fight and quarrel. (James 4:1–2)

At the root of so much of our anger and emotional volatility is our preoccupation with our own point of view and the prideful presumption—however subconscious—that our concerns are of primary importance in relationships, even within the marital context. It is no wonder that Paul writes, "Look not only to your own interests but to the interests of others" (Philippians 2:4).

Here is a healthy starting place to consider. Ephesians 4:29 offers, "Let no corrupt talk come out of your mouths but only such as is good for building up." Communication should always be constructive in the pursuit of understanding and in the practice of conflict resolution. In my opinion, as a rule of communication in marriage, this is a gamechanger, but it cries out against human nature and requires a certain God-assisted discipline for it to guide the discussions and dialogues of our lives together.

Let us examine how that might work for this couple who have been married for nineteen years. Parents of two children, ages fifteen and thirteen, both spouses are successful in leadership positions at work and have their own work lives outside marriage. Those responsibilities, coupled with their commitment to hands-on parenting and active service in the church they attend, create a labyrinth of scheduling conflicts and sit-down conversations about how to manage their lives. These discussions can provoke a myriad of emotions and often end poorly. Why? She is confrontational and a "fixer" wanting to always drill down to agreement and resolution whereas he is more easygoing and would be content to see how things play out. Consequently, he often withdraws from such conversations—if not physically then emotionally. He argues that he has enough of these situations to handle in his busy workday.

On this day, the discussion is about the budget. Although there is enough money, there is always the question about what the priorities in budgeting are and, specifically, in spending discretionary money or things not in the budget.

"I see you spent $500 on a new shotgun. I thought we had agreed our next thing to buy was a new stove. We both have said how costly our electric stove is and you know I have always wanted a gas stove. And you promised we would get one when I reluctantly agreed to buy this house two years ago. You always get what you want."

This starts out well with addressing an expenditure that seemed to contradict what his wife understood to be the priority. She does not voice opposition to the shotgun but to the departure of what she thought was the agreed-upon process of acquisition. She suggests this was something they both wanted or at least agreed was needed. But she struggles to conceal the reluctance she had in purchasing the house—now reawakened—and ends with a meant-to-be painful accusation. "You always get what you want."

"Ouch? Really? Who just bought a new computer for work when the old one worked perfectly fine?" He is suddenly engaged and now defensive with his own perception of how things really work in family finances. You can guess where it goes from here.

These kinds of conversations are a mainstay of everyday life. No matter how well-ordered the budget, or "perfect" the accounting, this kind of disagreement is probable. So what should she do? Should she bite her lips and say nothing? No, repressing and suppressing her feelings is not a healthy option. And what should he do when confronted? Should he say, "If that's how you feel, you handle the finances" and then leave the room to avoid further conflict? No, this only accelerates the burgeoning tension between them.

Communication should always be constructive in the pursuit of understanding and the practice of conflict resolution.

Here is a revised scenario with that principle in mind:

"Sweetheart, I was going through the checkbook and saw a check to Bill's Sporting Goods for a new shotgun. I know you have wanted one, but I was surprised you went ahead. I thought we were going to talk before we made out next big purchase."

"You're right. I should have talked to you first, but it was the last day of a closeout sale and it was 50 percent off and I could not resist. I used part of the bonus I got last month. Are you unhappy with me?"

"No, just disappointed. We have been talking the last few months about the kitchen stove and you know how much I want a gas stove. We have argued about it since the day we bought the house."

"I'm sorry. I guess I did not think. I know the stove is important, but I followed my greedy gut and got the shotgun. I am sorry. I have an idea. The leftover money from my bonus is more than enough to buy a new stove. Let us go out to dinner Friday after work—the kids both have plans—and then pick out a new stove. I guess it's about time."

"And maybe we should agree to talk before making major purchases so we stay on the same page. By the way, I have grown to like our house, and with a new gas stove, I might actually love it!"

This scenario may seem idealistic, unnatural, or even Pollyannaish. But why is that? Because we all too often act without thinking, argue without listening, and exit without resolving. What about the principle we are examining works here?

1. The issue is real. It is not ignored.
2. The confrontation is kind and not accusatory.

3. The response is honest and thoughtful.

4. The ensuing dialogue is reconciliation oriented.

5. The result is mutually satisfying and instructive.

What do we really want when we engage in confrontational dialogue? Do we want resolution in our conversations about conflict with our spouse? Thinking about that before we intentionally connect is critical to examining our motives. Are they really focused on the ultimate good of our relationship or are they a selfish attempt to get my own way? Discerning that may require stripping away layers of self-justification and rationalization, but the net effect of honest introspection of our motives can short-circuit the highly emotional, anger-fueling dialogue in which we unwittingly engage.

Here is an important principle: *the difference between reacting and responding is time.* In the moment when we encounter potentially emotionally disruptive conversations, it is difficult not to react. A *reaction* is often quick, given without much thought, and unfiltered. In contrast, a *response* is more often thoughtful, calm, and nonthreatening. In order to respond, an allocation of time may be necessary. For example, if you have just heard something that has induced a potentially defensive emotional reaction, you could begin by saying, "I want to think about what you just said so I can respond appropriately. I know this is important to you and it is to me too." The challenge here is that the emotional party may want to dig in and drill down to resolution, but the request for time to process has the potential for mitigating the acceleration of anger. Usually it is helpful to identify a time frame for response. "Let's eat dinner, and afterward we will sit down and talk about it."

The scriptural admonition at the beginning of this chapter emphasizes these truths. "Let no corrupting talk come out of your mouths but only such as is good for building up" (Ephesians 4:29).

1. There is *no* justifiable time or occasion that merits corrupt communication.
2. Contextually corrupt communication does not meet the criteria of "building up," encouraging, and resolving conflict.
3. The "let" implies we are not powerless in resisting the impulse to engage in self-serving demeaning dialogue.

As a practical follow-up to the consideration of our conflict-ordered communication, have you ever considered how much of your face-to-face dialogue is conflict resolution oriented as compared to encouraging and edifying one another. The pace of life tends to "honor" the tyranny of the urgent. We are preoccupied with work, parenting, and to-do lists, which are all good things, but they can diminish our opportunities for interfacing with healthy and constructive dialogue. We have to be intentional and set aside time to agree not to consistently rehearse the problems and daily challenges of our lives. Instead, we need to ask, "When can you and I have some downtime (fun time) together?" Or we need to ask, "How do you think we are growing in our relationship?"

Another helpful tool is what I identify as *reflective learning*. This is the intentional mindset that, following conflict and attempted resolution, whether successful or not, past the time and the emotion of the moment, asks, "How could we have done that better? What could I have said that would have been more constructive? What can we learn from that situation that will keep us from doing it again (if painful) or remind us in the future what works (if helpful)?"

Breaking the pattern or downward cycle of attempted conflict management gone bad requires intentionality and resolve. Anything we do on the backside of handling a conflict in a constructive way is worth celebrating and then embracing as a pattern for future resolution opportunity. Reflective learning can facilitate that process.

Conflict resolution is facilitated by a commitment to the use of constructive words geared toward a mutually beneficial end. In relationships, focusing on the "we" more than just the "me" is a critical motivation for choosing your words wisely. Learning together what works—and what doesn't work—can be instructive and keep us from fulfilling the notion that the only thing we learn from history is that we don't learn from history.

CHAPTER

5

As fits the occasion, that it may give grace to those who hear.

—EPHESIANS 4:29

*An intentional sensitivity to the specific circumstances
and needs of the communicant should shape
and frame how we talk with them.*

Circumstances often dictate the nature and, to some extent, the quality of our communication. In marriage we learn soon enough who is a morning person and who is not. We discover how a day at work affects our ability to assimilate at home.

Children challenge our reservoir of energy and our capacity for adaptation. The strain of financial responsibility and house and vehicle maintenance clamor for our attention. Coalescing multiple schedules and assessing priorities are part of our daily ware. And during it all, the "luxury" of discretionary resources like time and money are besieged with allocations for kids' sporting events, elusive vacation time, and church service projects.

How do we find time to talk?

We must first agree that talk is essential to growing and maintaining our relationship. For many couples, talk is moistly mandated by the tyranny of the urgent. Conflict often forces talk, and if conversations have been infrequent, the skill set for this kind of communication is probably underdeveloped. The situations that precipitate this kind of necessary dialogue tend to be in the moment, more often reactionary than anticipated. Already the grounds for misunderstanding and escalating tension are unwittingly being laid.

As a result of the multiple voices begging for our attention, the understanding of this principle is essential. An intentional sensitivity to the specific circumstances and needs of our spouse should shape and frame how we talk. The biblical reference for this is a continuation of Ephesians 4:29. "Let no corrupt talk come out of your mouths but only such as is good for building up." And this includes this completion of the thought: "as fits the occasion, that it may give grace to those who hear."

Remember the couple we introduced in the last chapter? They both work and have two teenage children. Their lives are insanely busy as they parse out time for their jobs, their kids, their kids' activities, their church, their social network, their infrequent personal recreation, the maintenance of their house, vehicles, stuff—and the list goes on. It may be why he bought the shotgun without talking to his wife first, precipitating the potential crisis we examined together earlier.

He is concerned about his wife's health and wants to share his feelings with her. She eats on the run, has no time for exercise, and has gained thirty pounds over the last year. She is still beautiful and desirable to him, but he is genuinely concerned about her health because her family has a history of heart problems; in fact, her father died of a heart attack before he was sixty because he was obese. These questions are racing through his mind. *Should I even mention this to her given her sensitivity about her weight? How could I communicate this in a loving nonjudgmental way? When would we even have time to have a meaningful conversation about this?*

All of these are the right questions. His other option is to wait and hope she figures it out while at the same time acknowledging his growing concern and agitation with what he sees happening. Putting off the conversation has made him increasingly distant because he does not want to upset her, but he is already upset. He decides that talking about it is the only real option. He cannot repress his feelings forever and already it is a battle to ignore them.

What about her circumstances are helpful for him to consider here?

- the busyness of her schedule
- her sensitivity and defensiveness about her weight
- her health and her genetic predisposition to weight and heart issues

Here is how he plans this confrontation:

- My goal is for her to eat better and feel better.
- I am willing to help her so the use of "we" in my suggestions is critical.
- I am going to wait until the weekend when we are less busy and take her on a date so the setting is optimal for dialogue.

The date night arrives, and here is a snapshot of the conversation:

"I am so glad for this time together—a break for us in the middle of our busy, nonstop lives. I am committed to making this happen more often. I am concerned as well about our general health. I am feeling my sixty-hour workweeks catching up with me, sleeping less, and too many fast-food meals at work. Are you having any of the same feelings?"

"I am. My schedule is crazy, our meals are more rushed, our exercise less frequent. How long has it been since we walked at the beach? And my clothes are getting tighter. Ugh."

"I have a proposal for you. Tell me what you think. For the

next thirty days, let us go on a 'Get healthy kick.' We will each set up some goals—target weight, days of exercise, and types of activity we can do together—and maybe we can just for the time adjust our portions and swear off fast food. And we hold each other accountable. How is that for a starting point?"

"I am afraid of failing, but I suppose we could try. I know I feel better when I am exercising and eating right."

"We are in this together, and I give you permission to remind me when I am getting careless. Do you want me to do the same for you?"

You are probably scratching your head and saying, "We could never have this kind of conversation." And it probably will not go as smoothly as this. But if your intent is to build up and encourage while at the same time confronting an issue, this template for how to choose your words wisely can help shape your important discussions about things that matter.

In formulating constructive dialogue, particularly in addressing conflict, what does it mean "as fits the occasion"? This literally means "good for edifying of need—meeting a particular need in view" (Desiring God). When confronting your spouse about an issue that is a potential conflict, it is imperative to ask yourself, "Whose need am I addressing?"

Two and a half years ago, I felt was at an impasse with my wife over whether we should move on to her son's property. It was a beautiful place, a good spot for us in our semiretirement, and it clicked a lot of buttons for my wife, who was excited about being near four of her grandchildren. I had reservations about privacy and was still hopeful we might find our own house so we spent six months dialoguing about this move. Her son was patient while we debated the pros and cons. We would say to each other, "Make your best argument," and then listen to the other poignantly make their presentation. We had determined together we would not move unless we agreed.

What motivated me in the end was this: "How could I meet this need/desire for my spouse wholeheartedly and embrace it as my own?" It was not as if the option was unattractive or frightening. I just had my own ideas about where I wanted to live when we had moved to the Central Coast four years earlier. My wife was sensitive to that, patient, and not demanding. She vacillated herself in the process, but the day came when I said to her, "Let's make the move." What tipped the scales for me in making that decision? It was so important to her it became equally important to me and my minor reservations were swallowed up by my commitment to our mutual happiness— something that decision has worked to positively shape our senior years.

We could still be in the rental today, away from our family, with me selfishly holding out for something probably unattainable, at an impasse, because I was unwilling to see the need as our need and refused to give in. Such decisions are exercises of grace and require listening to each other and, in the end, listening to our hearts.

John Piper said, "All our speech is to be a display of grace" (Desiring God). What arena demands that more than marriage? To manage this on our own is difficult, if not impossible. Earlier in Ephesians 4:21–24, Paul wrote,

You have heard about Him and were taught in Him, as the truth is in Jesus to put off your old self, which belongs to your former manner of life and is corrupt through deceitful desires and to be renewed in the spirit of your minds and to put on the new self, created after the likeness of God in true righteousness and holiness.

What is in focus here is the ongoing work of God in us shaping and molding us to become husbands and wives who live and talk together in ways that honor Him. God has begun that work in us as believers and intends to complete it Philippians 1:9. Marriage challenges us to give grace to one another—we both need it—just as we receive His grace daily, because we are bankrupt without it.

Here are some possible discussion topics for you to have together:

1. How often and how well do we tackle difficult topics?
2. Is it safe for us to tell each other how we feel about things when we disagree?
3. Is there a better time for us to have meaningful discussions about hard issues?
4. How well do I exercise grace when I am engaged in dialogue about topics that are potentially divisive?
5. What are ways I can demonstrate sensitivity and grace when initiating or responding to conflicting ideas?

Choosing your words wisely in resisting the expression of any unwholesome or corrupt communication and resolving to verbalize what is edifying and appropriate for your spouse's needs as a means of grace to him/her, with a mutual commitment that she/he will do that with/for you, can transform a marriage.

6

Be kind to one another, tenderhearted.

—EPHESIANS 4:32

Kindness in communication is never optional.

Kindness seems to be the missing element in current communication. There is a growing sense of acrimony and anger in critical venues, including politics, religion, family structure, morals, and values—all the stuff that really matters in life. We subconsciously are forced to have predetermined boundaries—even in some of our closest relationships—about what we will and will not talk about, even if not discussed beforehand. Maybe this works in most relationships, but it does not work in marriage. Unfortunately, this is often the norm of conduct in marriage, the most intimate of relationships. And this pattern of dysfunction often stimulates the destructive cycle of communication that undermines marriage.

Why is it so difficult to talk about the things in which we have differing ideas and opinions? At the crux of the issue is this principle: *meaningful mature relationships are characterized by a "safe place" for sharing our deepest feelings.* How then does kindness contribute to the dynamics of healthy communication in the marriage relationship?

It is important to say that *kindness in communication is never optional.* The biblical imperative from Ephesians 4:32 is "Be ye kind one to another, tenderhearted." In the next chapter, we will deal with the second part of this critical verse that provides a foundation for our focus on the importance of choosing your words wisely.

Let us define two important terms at the outset. *Kindness* may seem like a relatively benign word for us, but in terms of practical implementation, it is obviously more complex. A general definition today includes the idea of having empathy and sympathy, rooted in the earlier ideas of being affectionate and loving. In the biblical context, the root Greek word meant "serviceable, good, pleasant, gracious" (Vines). *Tenderhearted* expands that concept to the state of being easily internally moved to love, pity, and even sorrow. The idea of pity in this definition is not a condescending idea but more one of genuine sadness.

In this chapter, that is meant to be practical since the

importance of kindness is probably one we would universally acknowledge. I want to share seven principles that effectively impact kindness in the ways we communicate with each other, ensuring a "safe place" to share our true feelings.

1. "Dumping my garbage" on my spouse is not communication.

More than once in my counseling practice, I have heard someone indignantly protest, "But I told her exactly what I was thinking." The presumption in this statement is that somehow this represents communication. Generally, these kinds of "communications" are usually monologues designed to get something off one's chest without filters and without interest in any kind of response. Such "communication" is seldom productive, and often it is unkind without any consideration of how it might impact the listener.

The contemporary idea that declaring what we think and how we feel is good is often unilateral in its enactment. Hence the idea it is merely "dumping our garbage" without any consideration of the stench it leaves in its wake is overlooked.

Kindness demands that whenever we are contemplating sharing our deepest feelings in a context we consider "safe," we must consider how what we have to say will potentially impact our spouse. Consistent with that mindset, we will choose wisely the words we use. We may preface them with a statement like this: "I want to share something that has been on my mind for some time. I just want you to listen, and hopefully, you can better understand how I feel and we can talk about it together. Your opinion matters to me."

Being kind demands this type of foresight and acknowledgment so that the internal ways we feel and the important things we think have the goal of mutual understanding, if not appreciation.

2. The use of "I feel" statements is a red flag to the other for active listening.

Statements like "You love your work more than you love me" create a response of certain defensiveness. No person would openly admit that was a true statement. It dies a short death because it short-circuits dialogue. In this instance, consider this approach: "I know you don't mean it, but when you come home from work and immediately get on your cell phone, it makes me feel as if your work is more important to you than I am."

Blatant, unfiltered declarations tend to be hurtful and unkind, whether intended or not. Generally, they are birthed in a moment of mounting frustration and are often the result of triggering something that has been stored away via repression and suppression. It is the steam kettle effect. Things have been brewing and boiling, and now in a moment when the emotional guard is down, what comes bursting out is brutally honest but painful and harmful to hear.

The commitment to use "I feel" statements presupposes that your spouse is interested in your feelings. If that does not matter to your spouse, there are deeper issues to consider. I encourage couples to use statements that begin with "I feel" as a red flag—not a danger signal but a signal to listen carefully. Remember feelings are neither right nor wrong. They are what they are, but owning them and identifying them to your spouse presupposes that sharing them with the goal of greater understanding and potential reconciliation when hurt has been incurred is a worthwhile pursuit. Choosing your words wisely in expressing your feelings is a critical part of effective communication.

3. Validation of feelings—not defensiveness—creates a platform for ongoing dialogue.

The first response to "I feel" statements is validation. It is important to remind yourself that validation is not the same as agreement (i.e., that the way your spouse feels is good, healthy, or warranted from your point of view). It is the recognition that the feelings expressed are real for the communicant and need to be acknowledged as such.

A kind response is meant to be intentionally empathetic or sympathetic (e.g., "I am sorry you feel that way" and "Is there something I can do to help you?"). If the feelings expressed are negative and have to do with your behavior, respond with something like "I am sorry. What did I say or do that caused you to feel like that?"

Our natural tendency is to defend ourselves against the idea that we are the source of someone's discomfort or duress.

But that ignores the impact of our words and actions, no matter how well-intended. If being "tenderhearted" means being easily moved internally by our love for someone, our first intentional response should not be to protect our own feelings but to acknowledge the feelings of our spouse. Validation creates a platform for continuing dialogue that defensiveness inhibits. Choosing the way we respond to "I feel" statements is critical in pursuing productive and healing dialogue.

4. The primary goal of communication should be understanding, not agreement.

One of the factors that undermines healthy dialogue about conflict is our fixation with agreement over understanding. Agreement in conflict is facilitated by understanding each other's point of view. But agreement does not need to be the goal of every discussion about conflict. Agreement suggests that it is essential that we either compromise or abandon a point of view that is important to us. In some situations, that is necessary, such as "Shall we have another child?" and "Is moving across the country a good idea?"

Understanding, on the other hand, is more about developing an appreciation for each other's point of view and not demanding capitulation to ours. Remember the illustration I shared about moving on to my wife's son's property? We spent a considerable amount of time making our best arguments, seeking to persuade and understand each other, committed to not moving forward until or if we agreed.

Again, some situations require agreement in the moment, but in these discussions, giving attention to understanding each other's perspective should be the common denominator in the decision-making process.

I am confessing that there are too many conversations I have when I want my wife to agree. And I can drill down with my most persuasive—sometimes manipulative—arguments for my point of view without really caring what she thinks. This is a formula for stress and tension. Choosing the mindset and the right words in this kind of communication motivated by a tender heart accelerates the potential for harmony, even agreement.

5. Understanding each other's speed of processing information is critical to healthy communication.

We all process information differently. I am by nature an overt processor. I like to verbalize what I am thinking, and sometimes I choose to journal because it is important for me to get my thoughts outside me. Sharing my thoughts may not always be what my wife wants to hear in the moment.

I also am a "fixer" by nature and because of my work as a counselor. I want to "fix" everything, solve every problem, identify a course of action, etc. This can negatively impact the communication process with my spouse. Sometimes she comes to me with information and my immediate reaction is to go into "fix it" mode when all she wants is for me to listen. Cognizant of that, I have learned to ask, "Do you want me to be a listener, or do you want me to provide feedback?" We smile in those moments because she understands my natural propensity for wanting to fix things. But it works to help us process the things she wants to share with me.

Some people are internal processors. They need more time and want to think about the conversation in question more deeply and deliberately on their own. It is helpful in the marital relationship, if this is the case, for the more deliberate processor to say, "I need more time to think about this." And then, because the "fixer" is on tiptoes waiting for a response, it is helpful to set a time to return to that conversation. "Maybe we can talk more about this after dinner" or "I know this is important to you and I promise to respond to you before the day is over."

The manner and speed in which we process information is fertile ground for conflict unless in kind consideration for one another we recognize that one manner of processing is necessarily better than another. We can acknowledge it is simply how we are each hardwired. We will then choose our words wisely in how we enter and exit conversations when we are seeking dialogue and feedback.

6. "Mirroring" aloud what we have heard our spouse say allows for greater understanding.

Some of my clients suggest their spouse has selective hearing or convenient amnesia. Hopefully, they are smiling when they say this. It is not uncommon to interpret a message differently from how it was intended or to forget something said to us because it was less important to us than the messenger communicated. This is not necessarily a bad thing if we can acknowledge our human frailty and mutually determine how to limit these occurrences.

In counseling couples through crisis, I often wonder whether they were in the same room when a reported conversation was taking place. How can such a dichotomy between information given and received happen?

Sometimes we are simply too preoccupied, emotionally involved, or absent to listen well. Sometimes the method in which the communication is given—screaming, crying, accusing, berating—makes listening impossible. In any case, even with the best of intentions, we can misinterpret what was said to us in a moment of important communication.

Here are a few suggestions for situations like this: Begin by saying, "This is really important for me for you to hear." This is a signal for your spouse to pay attention. Selecting the time to have important discussions, as much as is possible, is critical to the process as well, so on the way to the neighbor's house for dinner with the children in the car may not be the best time.

As a respondent in this kind of dialogue, it is helpful to respond after listening by saying, "This is what I think I heard you say." This opens the door for continuing conversation and dialogue about the issue being considered. In utilizing such tools for being on the same page in conversations, it may feel awkward, if not contrived, at first. But incorporating these techniques in mirroring what the other has said contributes to enhanced memory and understanding.

7. Changing the patterns of communication that cause our conversations to cycle downward requires intentionality.

A lot of counseling I do has to do with communication issues, often involving conflict resolutions skills or the lack of them. It is easy to get locked into a pattern of dysfunctional communication, and once it starts, each party assumes their familiar role; inevitably it cycles downward to a place of frustration and hurt. I often say, "Someone has to break the cycle," or "Someone needs to alter the pattern of conflict resolution." You cannot keep doing the same thing and expect different results.

This husband and wife argue a lot. The pattern of communication looks like the following. Notice the cycle downward.

Husband (accusation): "You forgot to put gas in my car again."

Wife (defensive): "After all I've had to do this week, I can't believe you would complain about that."

Husband (selfish): "And I guess my sixty hours of work this week to pay the bills doesn't count for anything?"

Wife (defensive): "And I guess taking care of three kids and homeschooling them is no big deal either."

Husband (authoritarian): "The last thing I told you this morning when you borrowed my car was to put gas in it. How difficult is that?"

Husband (angry): "It's clear to me that all you care about is your precious car and my hard work at home is the last thing on your mind."

Wife (dismissive): "Whatever. The next time you ask to use the car, remember this conversation."

How did this married couple end up here? We are not even considering his slamming of the door as he exits the house and her painful crying as she returns to getting the children ready for school. Notice the downward cycle of their conversation. There is no kindness. There is no validation of feelings. There is no attempt at understanding. There is no exiting the process without inflicting pain upon one another.

Sadly, they have been doing this for ten years. This pattern of communication has doomed them to a life of emotional duress and inevitable distancing from one another. If he had simply said, "Honey, did you forget to put gas in my car?" And if she had responded, "I am so sorry. In the hassle of getting the kids to their ball games on time, I guess I forgot." And then maybe there is a remedy to be pursued. For example, she offers, "Why don't you use my car and I'll get gas for you today?" Or he responds, "No worries. I know you have been busy. I'll leave a few minutes early and stop on the way to work and fill it up."

Stepping out of painful patterns of communication demands a searching of our hearts. Ideally, there must be a mutual commitment to changing the process; at the very least, one party needs to determine, "I will not react the way I usually act. I will find a way to respond appropriately."

Let me remind you again of one additional tool. It is what I call reflective learning. When you have had an unsavory, painful conversation that you manage to painfully resolve, sleep on it. But in the days ahead, when the dust has cleared and emotions have waned, revisit that situation. In a moment of "tenderheartedness," say to your spouse, "What happened Thursday night was painful, wasn't it? How could I have handled it differently?" Or say, "What can we learn from our scuffle last week that will help us not repeat it next time?" Take some time reflecting on it. You will probably be able to smile—even laugh about it—because of your renewed mutual commitment to choose your words wisely in your future conversations.

7

Forgiving one another as God in Christ forgave you.

—EPHESIANS 4:32

*Practice forgiveness towards one another
as Christ modeled it towards you.*

The admonition to "be kind to one another, tenderhearted" is expanded in Ephesians 4:32 to include "forgiving one another as God in Christ forgave you." I suspect that this may be the greatest challenge of all because it may seem unnatural, unwarranted, and at the very least, unsustainable in the sense of its practical implications. In the intentional practice of choosing your words wisely, however, this will force a careful examination of your motivation and methodology in communicating with your spouse, especially in times of confrontation and conflict.

The model for this kind of behavior assumes we adhere to the teaching of the Bible and that the picture of God's forgiveness of us should prompt us to pursue the same in our relationship with others. I am aware that not everyone reading this will share a common faith, and the final chapter hopefully will attempt to address that disparity. However, it is my conviction that this principle is universally applicable. An awareness of our own brokenness should prompt grace and accommodation for another's failure.

No matter how good our intentions may be, we each possess the capability of hurting the one we love. How can that happen? In the introduction, we talked about the biblical question "How is it possible that cursing and blessing can come from the same fountain?" Or how can hurtful words come from a heart committed to our spouse? The simple answer is that we are all flawed and broken. Does that surprise you?

In today's counseling community, several ideas are central to the philosophical approach taken in addressing behavioral issues. The first is that we are impacted for good and/or bad by our family history and by our environment. Secondly, and there is debate about this, we are born essentially good—or at least with a blank slate—and make choices in how we respond based upon how we are impacted by genetic, psychological, and environmental factors that will determine ultimately who we are based on how we respond to these. This is obviously a simple generalization but represents some of the thinking that drives contemporary psychology and therapy.

In my counseling practice, I am often dealing with people who are painfully aware of their own brokenness or at least that of their spouse. The origin of that may be traced to a multiple of factors alluded to above and, in my belief system, to the sin and brokenness with which all of us enter the world. Suffice it to say, we arrive at relationships carrying whatever brokenness we have with us. Within that lies the propensity for causing pain even to the ones we love. It is not surprising to say, "We only hurt the ones we love."

Let us acknowledge then that we have the capacity for hurting one another, and that is probably most common in how we communicate with each other. If that is the case, how do we resolve those situations in which we have engaged in painful dialogue? Maybe we have observed most of the principles suggested but still fail miserably in achieving healthy conflict resolution. Anger erupts, harsh words are spoken, and damage is done. What then?

A kind and tenderhearted mindset does not guarantee we will be successful in constructive and healing conversation every time. It will, I believe, minimalize the incidents of such failure. It is possible, given all the other things going on in our lives, kind and tenderhearted words may be forfeited in a moment of escalating stress and tension. When the anger subsides, we are frequently left with a horrible, sick feeling in our stomachs. The challenge of how to reengage with our spouse, having exited poorly and painfully, is before us. To ignore such hurtful confrontations is not a healthy option, though often this seems the easiest path to follow. This can get stored away for the next confrontation and can be easily triggered when not resolved.

"I am sorry" and "I forgive you" are two expressions that provide healing and hope for relationship protection and preservation. Why are these two phrases so important?

"I am sorry" signals several important things. First, "I am taking ownership of the hurt caused by the words I said to you." Second, "I love you and would never intentionally want to hurt you." Finally, "I am not excusing or justifying my behavior." These are critical components of the reengagement process. Even though we may think we are right, we cannot sanction hurtful words and painful rhetoric used to make our point or to express our feelings. That acknowledgment is essential to having any hope of rebounding after conversations that effectively estrange us from one another. We should always be sorry when we have caused one another pain with the words we have chosen. But we should not foolishly assume everything is now all right, although the seeds for reconciliation have been sown.

"I forgive you" helps complete the cycle of healing. What does it mean to forgive? One idea is giving up my right to hurt you for hurting me. Forgiveness in the Bible is "a release or a dismissal of something" (Got Questions?). Forgiveness is letting go of the painful hurt caused me, so I will not be held hostage by its potentially bitter hold.

And why would I do this? I would choose to do this (it is usually not our first response) because I am aware of my own brokenness and my capacity for hurting others even when my intentions are honorable. I would also choose to do this because I do not want to remain emotionally estranged from my spouse. I want to be reconciled to him/her. Finally, I choose to do this because the pain of unresolved conflict leads to bitterness and resentment and that is too high a price to pay to maintain my position of being "in the right."

Here are some principles to think about in the "I am sorry" and "I forgive you" context:

1. It is important to identify what you are sorry for.

There is much debate about apologizing for what we are not sorry for. In conflict we may staunchly defend our position, even how we have couched our words, feeling that we chose them wisely. In the end, however, if what we have said caused pain, or if how we said it was hurtful because it was unfiltered, angry, or reactionary, then we should be motivated to say, "I am sorry." In checking our motivation, we may be convinced that what we said came from a good heart. However, we may acknowledge as well our methodology was flawed; there may have been a better way to say it.

Let me add here that it is possible that motive and method may not be the issue here; instead, there is unresolved stuff—even baggage—in our spouse's history or our own that is easily triggered. Being made aware of that in reflective dialogue can instruct us moving forward. Ideally this would shape how we communicated about this subject in future conversations. Armed with this information, we could then choose to use our words more wisely.

2. It is helpful to remember that a lack of closure from past hurts fuels and triggers the opportunity for ongoing pain.

A husband was listening to his wife rehearse something she had read in a magazine. Without thinking, he blurted out, "That's idiotic!" Immediately she broke into tears and left the room. Mystified, her husband pursued her to the bedroom, where she had barricaded herself. "Honey, I am sorry for what I said," he whispered through the door. He was uncertain about what would have caused such a response but was sorry for the apparent hurt caused her. In a few moments, she opened the door and confessed, "I know you didn't mean it, but my father called me an idiot every time I did something as a child and when I hear that word it reminds me of how stupid I am." He hugged her, apologized, and said, "I promise never to use that word again. You know I would never have used that word if I knew how hurtful it was to you."

That is the kind of baggage we bring into marriage, and our life experiences may cause painful issues to resurface. In such cases, we must listen and learn from one another. It is kindness—indicative of empathy and sympathy—that compels such healing dialogue.

To ignore hurtful words and behaviors in marriage is to ensure the ongoing potential for triggered painful communication. Earlier we talked about "keeping short accounts" through the appropriate expression of our feelings, especially our anger.

3. Forgiving and forgetting are often not on the same timeline.

When we have had a painful exchange of words that has cycled downward to unkind dialogue, "I am sorry" and "I forgive you" help initiate healing. Sometimes, however, when the behavior has been repeated, the intentional act of forgiving may not be accompanied by an immediate forgetting of what took place. "Forgive and forget" are not chronologically wed; in fact, when an ensuing similar conversation takes place, one of you may remind the other of the last time you had this conversation and how poorly it went. "I told you I was sorry." "Yes, but I haven't forgotten …"

The act of forgiving an offense committed against us is a choice we make. It is not an excusing of the hurtful words or behavior; rather, it is the acknowledgment of an apology and a decision to be gracious (sometimes owning our own propensity for painful words), accepting it in pursuit of the reconciliation essential to maintaining a healthy marriage.

The idea of "forgetting"—or not remembering it as a reference point for future conversations—may require extended discipline so that when the feeling of hurt reemerges I can say to myself, "But I have chosen to forgive him/her." This pattern of self-talk can lay the foundation for a different reference point from the hurt incurred.

4. There is a significant difference between forgiveness and reconciliation.

What if the words exchanged in a heated argument are so painful that it feels impossible to offer forgiveness to your spouse, much less forget what was said?

Every time this couple talks about their families, the husband has something critical to say about how his wife was raised and how it is affecting her parenting. This is hurtful to her on several levels since she is extremely sensitive. She has told him more than once when he has smugly said, "You sound just like your mother." He knows that is hurtful to her because she has explained how little love and attention her mother gave her growing up and how abandoned by her she feels now.

The children are fighting again when he comes home from work and his first words to her entering the kitchen are "Are you ever going to be different than your mother?" His wife, overwhelmed by a day of conflict with the children, reacts by saying, "You knew where I came from. You should never have married me." And with that, sobbing, she runs from the kitchen.

He is immediately sorry for what he said. Gathering

himself, he shouts to her, "Honey, I didn't mean that! I am sorry!"

She sleeps in the spare bedroom that night, and in the morning, as her husband approaches to embrace her, she says, "I forgive you, but I am going to need some time to deal with this." He insists, "But I said I was sorry." She responds, "You have said so many before, and though I want to believe you, I am not sure I can believe you." She has expressed a willingness to forgive but acknowledged reconciliation is a work in progress.

The next principle is important in understanding how to link forgiveness to reconciliation.

5. When there is a repetition of hurtful behavior, repentance is the key to reconciliation.

Our context for discussing forgiveness and reconciliation is confined more to words than behavior. For example, we are not talking about physical abuse, addictive behaviors, sexual impropriety, and failure. In these the process of reconciliation looks much different.

But in the case of hurtful dialogue—even verbal abuse—repentance may be critical to reconciliation. In the biblical context, repentance includes not only remorse but a change of mind and behavior—a change of direction. How does that work?

Our wife we've been referring to has heard repeated, "I am sorry," from her husband. She suspects he means it in the moment, but his recurrent behavior makes here skeptical about how sorry he is. As a result, she holds a little of herself back from him so that when the next night he wants to be intimate, she says, "I am not ready for that; just hold me."

Inwardly he may be thinking, *I thought she forgave me,* but it is important for him to come to grips with the fact he cannot keep speaking disparagingly about her mother when he gets angry. If this is hurtful to her, he must repent—not only be sorry for what he said but resolved to not say it again. Sometimes true reconciliation awaits repentance as evidenced in changed behavior.

This husband can facilitate the process of reconciliation in several ways, including being more proactive in helping with the children, complimenting Sarah when she is parenting well, and asking how he can ease her load when she seems overwhelmed. As he begins to choose his words wisely, all these things can demonstrate a change of direction leading to full reconciliation.

6. Forgiveness provides a freedom from the hurt and pain caused by our brokenness.

When we hold on to painful words and rehearse hurtful conversations, we are held in bondage to them. They cast a shadow on our marriage, and even though we may try to dismiss them, they begin to feed bitterness and resentment. If we cannot say, "I am sorry," when we have caused hurt or respond with "I forgive you" when an apology has been offered, we are choosing to prolong the pain that comes from unresolved conflict.

There is a certain freedom that comes from the act of forgiveness. Forgiveness may first be an intellectual decision, but in the end, it brings emotional healing. Each occurrence of failure reminds us of our brokenness and each decision to participate in the reconciliatory process has the potential for strengthening our marriage and diminishing our failure to choose our words wisely. The benefits of freedom from inner turmoil and unprocessed anger can be so compelling that the impetus to practice forgiveness in response to a genuine apology becomes a high priority.

7. Wisdom is seeing things from God's point of view.

I am closing this chapter with this statement taken from a Bill Gothard seminar I attended fifty years ago. It is easy to try to reckon with the multiple challenges of marriage with our own limited resources, unaware that they may sabotaged by our own history and brokenness. It is often hard to be objective in assessing what is wrong and why we react and respond the way we do.

I have always relied on the value of others' advice and wisdom. As a young pastor, I sought more seasoned ministers to give me counsel. Even now I have several older friends I share with when I am looking for perspective and wisdom.

My faith in God and in His Word—the Bible—is my

primary source of wisdom. Since I see God as my Creator and as the Sustainer of my life, I seek counsel from Him. I believe in the wisdom of the teaching of the Bible that has informed much of what I have written in this book.

In the final chapter, I want to share with you why this has been so important to me in my journey to choose my words wisely.

Conclusion

FROM PAPER TO PRACTICE

The principles I have presented have value for everyone. The focus of this book has been on the application of these principles by couples within the context of marriage. I am convinced, however, that these principles are valid and viable for anyone involved in a relationship worth preserving—with a family member, a fellow worker, a close friend, etc. It is possible as well that these principles could provide help for the mitigation of all kinds of interpersonal conflict due to the utility of effective communication. Even in the professional workplace where people are cohabitating shared space and coworking on projects that demand like-mindedness and mutual respect, there is potential benefit in evaluating these principles.

I am aware of my Christian background and the critical role my view of scripture—the Bible—plays in my thinking and counseling. I have not suggested that the panacea for every problem is to read your Bible and pray. If you have read this with a predetermined skepticism about the biblical perspective

I have chosen, it has probably made these principles seem almost simplistic, if not idealistic. But I would offer that these principles are not easily or even naturally applied; rather, they are sustainable only when accompanied by divine assistance.

The "Twelve Step" program of AA requires the recognition of a "higher power" for the addicted drinker, and the principles of the Bible—often diametrically different from the communicant's natural way of resolving conflict—require divine help beyond our own resources to break from addictive patterns of conduct and communication.

In summary, choosing your words wisely is accomplished through a blend of personal intentionality, mutual accountability, and spiritual alignment with the grace and strength God provides.

In the introduction, I referenced a portion of the Bible from James 3:13–18. I suggested five things I felt were important and foundational for this book. Let us examine them more closely here.

1. Wisdom and understanding are highly desirable.

Wisdom is acquired through listening to others potentially learning from our own life experiences and failures. Wisdom can also be gleaned from reading and then applying the things we discover in our search for understanding how to improve the quality of our relationships. Because healthy relationships are critical to experiencing a full life, the pursuit of wisdom in expanding our life resources should be a high priority.

The Bible is the true source of wisdom. I have relied on it throughout my life, and I reference frequently its practical truths in my counseling and coaching. The Bible says this about its repository of wisdom: "But the wisdom from above is first pure, then peaceable, gentle, open to reason, full of mercy and good fruits, impartial and sincere" (James 3:17). All the modifying words ascribed to "wisdom from above" are highly desirable components of meaningful communication. A spouse whose motive is pure and unselfish, whose method is peaceable, gentle, and open to reason, whose manner is full of mercy and good fruits, impartial and sincere, invests in a good result.

2. Our conduct—words and deeds—reflects our wisdom or lack of it.

"Who is wise and understanding among you? By his good conduct let him shows his works in the meekness of wisdom" (James 3:13). In the context of this chapter of the Bible, "works" refers to decisions we make about the words we choose and the actions we take.

There must be a connection between what we say we believe is true and important and subsequent conduct we embrace. If I say I believe that my role as a husband is to love my wife and to be willing to lay my life down for her (Ephesians 5:21–32), then I would never intentionally choose to hurt her. When confronted with my offenses against her—whether intended or not—my mindset should be to apologize for the hurt caused, to choose different words, and to change damaging behaviors.

Persistence in painful patterns of communication reflects a lack of humility—not owning my failure—and an unwillingness to align my conduct with the "meekness of wisdom."

3. Jealousy and selfish ambition are twin roots of unwise and hurtful conduct: words and deeds.

At the core of who we are resides the propensity for how we inappropriately view ourselves and others. The Bible calls this condition "sin" and identifies it as the universal condition of all men, keeping us from becoming the best version of ourselves. In psychological terms, we understand that the greater the tendency toward narcissistic behavior, the lesser the capacity for empathy. More simply stated, the greater our need for self-gratification, the less our ability to consider the needs of others.

Paul writes about this in his letter to the church at Philippi.

> Do nothing from selfish ambition or conceit but in humility count others more significant than yourselves. Let each of you look not only to his own interests but also to the interests of others. (Philippians 2:3–4)

There is a necessary and healthy care of our own needs that is essential. We must look to our own interests but not to the exclusion of others. Jealousy—being envious of what someone else has—and selfish ambition—wanting what I want no matter the potential cost and impact upon others—are twin components of painful behaviors and hurtful communication.

It may be our natural tendency to defend ourselves as an extension of justifying our word and actions, but relationships are built upon an intentional and determined consideration of how what we do and say affects those in our sphere of influence in private and in public places. For this we need God's help—the "wisdom that is from above."

4. Wisdom "from above" is reflected in the "good fruit" it bears.

Our "wisdom," if left to our own devices, will be short-circuited by our limitations and tend to be self-preserving. Even the wisdom of political pundits, contemporary philosophers, spiritual gurus, medical personnel, and well-meaning family and friends can be misleading. Though well-intended, it may simply ignore the obvious and reflect its own self-preserving mindset. A client's father felt that allowing others to help him in times of need would make him obligated ("beholding" was his word), so he counseled his son never to form any close relationships that would require him to return anything in kind. My client was lonely and depressed, locked out of any meaningful friendships. How wise was his father's counsel?

The "wisdom from above" identified by James is from God, found in His Word. Proverbs 3:5–6 instructs us to "lean not on your own understanding. In all your way acknowledge Him and He will make straight your paths." Seeing things from God's perspective—exploring the timeless truths of His Word—exposes us to life-changing principles such as those in this book. They are rooted in scripture, and when applied and practiced with God's grace and strength, they produce the "good fruit" of healthy relationships.

5. Those who make peace sow and reap a harvest of righteousness (right living).

"Why can't we all just get along?" That seems like an appropriate refrain in a day of tension and conflict. Everywhere we look we observe the ravages of jealousy and selfish ambition. We want what everyone else has and we do not have, and we will chase it without respect of the route we take and the people we injure. This blindness blunts our ability to see our own faults and, not surprisingly, magnifies the shortcomings of others. Jesus asked, "Why do you see the speck in your brother's eye but do not notice the log in your own eye?" (Matthew 7:5).

What if our goal in relationships was always to maintain or make peace? What if our deepest desire in marriage was to live in harmony with our spouse? What if we were committed to communicating in a way that affirmed and validated rather than critiqued and berated? If peace is our objective, we must sow seeds of kindness, tenderheartedness, and forgiveness. We do that most effectively with the words that we intentionally use to manage conflict, resolve problems, make decisions, embrace differences, and ultimately edify and honor one another.

The result—the "harvest"—is identified in James as "righteousness." In summarizing this, The Message relates this paraphrase of these verses:

> Real wisdom, God's wisdom, begins with a holy life and is characterized by getting along with others. It is gentle and reasonable, overflowing with mercy and blessings, not hot one day and cold the next, not two-faced. You can develop a healthy, robust community that lives right with God and enjoy its results only if you do the hard work of getting along with each other, treating each other with dignity and honor. (James 3:17–18)

Choosing your words wisely is not embarking on a quick-fix, seven-step program or pursuing a magical formula guaranteeing instantaneous results. It is, rather, the daily intentional pursuit of a lifestyle of speaking the truth in love to one another with the goal of caring for and honoring one another. In doing this, we can experience the richness and blessing of relationships that matter.

Printed in the United States
by Baker & Taylor Publisher Services